Northern Lights

NORTHERN/SOUTHERN HEMISPHERE

Grand Canyon

ARIZONA, USA

Great Barrier Reef

QUEENSLAND, AUSTRALIA

Victoria Falls

ZIMBABWE/ZAMBIA

Mount Everest

CHINA/NEPAL BORDER

Paricutin Volcano

MICHOACÁN, MEXICO

Yosemite

CALIFORNIA, UNITED STATES

Niagara Falls

NEWYORK AND ONTARIO, US & CANADA

Horseshoe Bend

ARIZONA, USA

Azure window

MALTA

Nā Pali Coast

KAUA'I, HAWAII ISLANDS

Pulpit Rock cliff

NORWAY

Giant's Causeway

NORTHERN IRELAND

Wadi Rum

JORDAN

Lake Baikal

RUSSIA

Banff National Park

CANADA

Salar de Uyuni

BOLIVIA

Yellowstone

WYOMING, UNITED STATES

Sahara Desert

NORTHERN AFRICA

Galapagos Islands

ECUADOR

Pamukkale

TURKEY

Zangjiajie National Forest

CHINA

Mount Bromo

INDONESIA

Halong Bay

VIETNAM

Amazon Rainforest

SOUTH AMERICA

Serengeti Migration

TANZANIA

Crater Lakes of Mt. Kelimutu

INDONESIA

Lake Titicaca

PERU

Grand Teton National Park

WYOMING, UNITED STATES

Viñales Valley

CUBA

Antelope Canyon

ARIZONA, UNITED STATES

Bisti Wilderness

NEW MEXICO, UNITED STATES

Nyiragongo Volcano

DR CONGO

Gros Morne National Park

CANADA

Stone Forest

CHINA

Colca Canyon

PERU

Tiger Leaping Gorge

CHINA

Drakensberg

SOUTH AFRICA

Huascaran National Park

PERU

Tianmen Mountain

CHINA

www.ingramcontent.com/pod-product-compliance
Ingram Content Group UK Ltd.
Pitfield, Milton Keynes, MK11 3LW, UK
UKHW060112300726
14090UKWH00002B/150

* 9 7 8 9 1 8 9 4 5 2 7 3 2 *